MW01253817

Too Much Love

*Anna
sorella

love
Gia Gatano*

Too Much Love

Gianna Patriarca

QUATTRO BOOKS

The publication of *Too Much Love* has been generously supported by
the Canada Council for the Arts and the Ontario Arts Council.

 Canada Council   Conseil des Arts
for the Arts   du Canada

 ONTARIO ARTS COUNCIL
CONSEIL DES ARTS DE L'ONTARIO

Author's photograph: Joseph Paczuski
Cover painting: Robert Marra
Cover design: Diane Mascherin
Editor: Beatriz Hausner
Typography: Grey Wolf Typography

Library and Archives Canada Cataloguing in Publication

Patriarca, Gianna
    Too much love / Gianna Patriarca.

Poems.

Issued also in an electronic format.

ISBN 978-1-927443-04-0

    I. Title.

PS8581.A6665T66 2012   C811'.54   C2012-903900-4

Published by Quattro Books Inc.
382 College Street
Toronto, Ontario, M5T 1S8
www.quattrobooks.ca

Printed in Canada

The generations are different,
the stars are different, the sun
absolutely different, I see it
in the fact that it doesn't recognize me.
I myself am another.
— Anna Maria Ortese (1914-1998)

This is my letter to the World
That never wrote to Me
— Emily Dickinson (1830-1886)

When the child leaves, and the window goes on looking
out on empty walls, you will sit and dream of old things,
and things that could never happen.
— LeRoi Jones (1934-)

for my daughter Gia Alexandra

Contents

Decipher Me

Too Much Love

And each day the gap narrows
and each day the fury grows
– Antonia Pozzi

time to
improvise the happiness
arrange an alibi
time to
go before the mirror
an anarchist

once again a relocation
postmarked
by the last third
of this life

the time that counts
the difference-maker
the weight-loser
the turn-it-all-around period
without blood

the poems are written
the child is grown

you are tangential
but you are loved

hold on

Decipher Me

women my age
adjust to the changes
become dangerous
defiant
against measured time
without compassion

reluctant hands
withstand
lay out the best sheets
rearrange the guest room
for the inevitable intruder
somnolent
in the preparation

we have waited
too long
misplaced our pencils

allowed squatters
in untenanted spaces

My Name Is Giovanna Berta

i get my names
from my two uncles
Giovanni and *Umberto*
one a soldier
the other
a *bonvivant*
one died of the clap
the other a bullet

grandpa
was a communist
with a dent in his skull
from the great war
his oldest son wore
a black shirt
in *Mussolini*'s clan
marched tall and proud
in those leather boots

my father was the youngest
a prisoner of war
in Sardinia
with the Americans
who had food
he learned to cook their meals
on that rocky
sheep-infested island
for more than a year

mamma was sixteen
when the Germans sent her
out, pail in hand
to fetch water from a well
while the air raids bombed
the countryside
the shrapnel has left scars

mamma met a soldier
from Sicily
married him in 44
he died in 46

my father loved her
later

i was born
when it was quiet
before the evacuation
the *terranuova*

i listen to her stories
continue battling
the contradictions
in my blood

Alterations

All but Death,
can be Adjusted
– Emily Dickinson

doctor Charming
has faith in my metabolism
it works fine
considering
takes my visa number
guarantees
a year from now
i will be a different
woman

doctor Charming
will sell me tools
to build a brand new me
delicious as my name
full of vowels
an Italian *gelato*
refreshing as the little
blue pills he prescribes
and the special lamp
to jazz up my moods

twelve short months

an eternity
from now
i will come into bud
a rare species
in a recovered garden
i will become
contemporary

the uncontaminated space
of fashionable lines

doctor Charming
is another fleeting distraction
another interruption
a brief shopping experience
i will not wear
with much success

Translating the Sea

i am so far from the sea
i dream of it constantly

mamma tells me
water is
a bad sign
so are teeth
don't dream of water or
teeth
or
flying

mamma spends hours
on the phone with
her sisters
their lives
their pain
their bank accounts

then they decode
the dreams

i lie
when she asks about mine
terrified
she will discover
how often i fly
over the ocean
dropping big white teeth
into the waves

Love Is Not Subtle

love never smoulders
it devours
consumes
inhabits
without ceremony

it does not offer
a poised expectation
of things to come
it slams the door
rattles the windows
lets you know
it is home

take it
it's all yours to squander
and amuse
to play with
and put aside

all yours to
come back to
on an indifferent night
full of rain

Half Moons

the moon has
nothing to be sad about
– Sylvia Plath

under the half moons
we hold back

waiting for
the eclipse
the full
round coin
of light

that easy slide
into another
doubt
another madness

a brand new
anger
a new vision
of dark

You Bring Home Another Love

someone loves you
because they love you
i welcome them
into my living room
pour the tea with lemon
slice the sweet cake
plump up the pillow

i fall in love
with your happiness
ease myself into
your contentment
fall in love
with your love

when i am almost
comfortable
almost sure
you move on
to the next amusement

If Only I Could

spare you the pain
the long conversations
the rationale
for the end of love

the other woman
the other man
the boiling pot of
misunderstandings

how to present happiness
on a serving dish
with sweets
caramels
nothing bitter

if only i could
send you off to camp
hoping for a summer
without rain

Comfort Me

will a prayer do
one prayer
a decade
from the crystal rosary
blessed in that special place
we went in busloads
every summer
lugging all those
serious sins

we unloaded
lost weight
came home
with a new peace
a feathery soul

i don't know how
to comfort you now
i cannot remember
the words that go with
the beads
i cannot distinguish
the sin
from the grace

Wrestling Again

pessimist soul
damned
mortal sins
must go to
confession

but i want to look at trees
today
read that book
on the useless sex
smoke another cigarette
write something about
love

we promised each other
we would be happy
remember

i want to fall in love
again
get it right

Silenzio

you spare me the truth
you think i rest better

what i don't know about you
is worse than
any truth

what i conjure in my head
can stop my heart

i count the mistakes
regrets
the words we
never spoke
when we should have

the absolute waste
of love disguised

the silence

At This Age

at this age
i love things
differently

without the need
to jump into the well
the deepest part of
the lake

i am drawn to the calm
the grace
of an ordinary day
my mother's hands

at this age
i applaud what is
foolish
absurd
i'm a spectator

how sweet now
the resistance
to argue

Another Visit with You

for my father

waiting for summer
hesitant season
trickster

magnolia branches
roughed up by wind
the sun acting bashful
headstones
polished by rain

the bench is still broken
so i sit on the cement
step around you
pull out the notebook
the black felt pen
twenty-eight years
and counting

another poem
you won't read
another cigarette
you can't deny me
another visit with you
and this useless
annoying fly
that won't leave
me alone

the first day of May
a good day to talk
a good day to write
a good day to put out
the smoke for good

Inheritance

when i was your nursemaid
your interpreter
drove you to all those doctors
resenting your pain
the way you laid it all on me
the oldest
the daughter
who knew the language best

i hated your pain
hated you
for being full of hurt

you were the man

i have inherited
your weaknesses
the bad knees
the fears

but my doctor's visits
are on my own

Birthday Poem Wish

my husband tries hard
to erase my sadness
and i become
more sad
because i cannot be happy
for him

Resisting the Underground

he keeps her in
the basement
safe underground
warm there
except in winter
when the cold sneaks
through the cracks

if he keeps her there
she will never leave
he thinks
even if she complains about
the dampness
the spider webs

she's not happy there
that low ceiling
the dust that settles
on everything
her breath struggling
but she stays

he keeps promising
to make it nice
raise the ceiling
paint the walls

if he lets her out
he's sure she'll leave
but she has been there
too long

there is a certain comfort
in the discomfort

she only wants the light
for a little while
just long enough
to dry the damp frayed linen

Love Disguised

after the romance
there is tolerance
or violence
the journalist
writes

so many uncertainties
half truths
between spoken lines
written lines
the headline

a suburban bungalow
in the month of March
a woman silenced
by knives

too much space
between Brampton
and Mumbai
not enough gold
to sanctify a marriage

veils too thin
to conceal deception

everywhere
stunning fabrics
disguised as love

Allow Me

i read somewhere
that poetry written
by women
is always
sub-standard
weak
unstructured
merely
sentimental
domestic at best

allow me the fantasy
the myth
that i can be part of
the chorus

i can step on the stage
and we can split the
applause

Gloria at LAX, Jan. 3, 2009

caught a glimpse of Gloria Steinem
at LAX by the Air Canada counter

her hair still parted in the middle
still honey coloured
thick
on her head full of thoughts

she is smaller in real life
tiny
delicate
beautiful

some things should never change
some people should never shrink

Now

words
solitude
pain

pathetic
silence
no longer
political

once
the angry pen
rejected the bully

now
it greets the quiet
neglecting politics
and poems

Mamma at 87

my mother's face returns
to the fireside
– Rocco Scotellaro

you've told me that story before
but i let you enjoy it again

you cry at the parts
you remember best
the easier times
so you say
even the war
under the airplanes
the hunger
that handsome soldier
with the mustache
your first love
Sicily
the widow you were
at twenty-two
that ship across the Atlantic
endless

sometimes you even remember
my father

you go on
another coffee
another fruit
a cracked walnut

your memories
my inheritance

*

after the talk
i move towards the door
i go and write
try to cheat death
with my words
gamble with time

but the cuffs are tight
on my wrists
like the sleeves of that
undersized uniform
the nuns made me wear
when you left me in their
company
all those years
when papa was away

you had to work
i needed someplace safe
you thought
but the nuns were just
a place

who will know me
this much
this way

i will write the stories
for you
one day

A Certain Day in May

Mrs. Arruda slipped out the side door
in her flannel nightgown
i watch her
from my kitchen window
as she surveys her garden
turning over a handful of soil
rubbing it into her palms
she smells it
tastes it
shaking her head

she looks at the sky
the clouds, the places where light
falls on her rectangular plot

i pour a cup of coffee
switch on the radio
CBC announces
Osama bin Laden
was killed today

i sip the coffee
open the window
my eyes settle on the spade
standing upright in the dirt
next to her rubber boots
by the water hose
the flowered scarf waits
pinned to the clothesline

the old woman stoops down
pulling out weeds
on the brick path

waiting to plant
something beautiful this month

that will grow strong and delicious
she will harvest with pride

needing to cultivate something
that has no connection
to terror

Reading the Women Who Loved

Sylvia Plath was
Lady Lazarus
baited by death

"Dying
is an art,"

she wrote

"like everything else,
I do it exceptionally well."

if life had been
a kinder lover
there would have been
more poems

*

you wonder why
we bother to love at all

time invested
touching
tears
lunacy in the end
wasted time

*

if i were honest
i would spell it out

poetry is a screen
for cowards

nightmares don't lie
they revisit with
the same vengeance
night after night
climb in your bed
stalking your sleep

you've hidden another body
killed someone else
your eyes open
you remove the blankets
look under the bed
convince yourself
it isn't there

what resilient creatures
we are
to endure it all
keep going

Irrelevant

Oh mother, please,
go write a poem about it…

my daughter dismisses the argument
with the quick flick of her slender
elegant hand

You are no longer relevant, deal with it

the all too pertinent voice of
Amy Winehouse on the stereo

no longer relevant

my young, beautiful
irresponsible daughter
deletes me with one short phrase
with the tap of the button
on the car radio

no, no, no!

look out
red light ahead
red light!

what do i do at a red light?

think, think
        red means …

i want to open the door
vanish into the night

but predictably i sit
hiding the hurt

just another insignificant
flesh wound
slightly larger than liver spots
barely noticeable

it is my daughter's world now
the discussion is over

my divine
indiscreet
self-absorbed child
adjusts her bra strap

The light's green mom!

i have stalled the car

Oh mother, not again!

i turn the key in the ignition
it won't cooperate
nothing is smoking
nothing on fire

Mom do something!

what to do?
what to do?

i am confused
mechanically challenged

the battery and me
both out of juice
and non-refundable

i close my eyes and pray
to Saint Anthony

my spawn
busy texting
couldn't be less interested
in me or the battery

i hope she has children one day

A Girl Made of Lavender

Clever Girl

they will reject you
clever girl you are
more than i imagined

you see things
in the daylight
i pretend
i live in the night

you are sure
my heart is blocked

an old fraud

you have seen through
its perforations
where it was gnawed

you confront the
impostor
sluggish muscle
without purpose

they will refuse you

this broken down
beating weight
tells me
they will be alarmed
by your truth

the god they
made me swallow
in thin
round
salt free
mouthfuls
will snub you

no status for your kind
among the chosen

the incense
the hymns
the communion
of things done right
you are all wrong

there is no place for me
either
at their table

i choose hell
before i deny you

*

you are stronger
than i will ever be
i claim some responsibility
for that
not the blood that runs
through our veins
type O positive
but all those nights
in my arms
in my bed
all the stories
poems

endless hours
with the oxygen mask
after the attacks
the tiny pills
that made your
heart race

you laughed through it all
held my hand
kept it steady

i am happy you are strong

The Boy Loves You

poured his heart out
after the third beer
the bottle of white wine
two *campari* and soda

the boy loves you
poor half-starved
unfortunate soul

said i had done
a good job
shouldn't blame myself

the boy wants to love you
forever
wants you to love him
forever

what can i do
i feed him
i listen
i mix the *campari* and soda

he's all wrong
but the boy loves you

The Words

i write the words because
my other jobs are done

they don't help much

between the complaints and
cramping hand
in the hours when i don't sleep
the words are my vodka
and gin

put pain in a waiting room
walk away
have another black coffee
forget they lied

beauty doesn't free you

Keats was lucky
he died young

before the truth

Accept Me

you need to construct
a demon to rebel against

i am perfect
he is perfect
we are your
perfect monster
i understand

i fought my own
long before you were
a consideration

you find it all
so comical

Just Be

Each to his grief, each to
his loneliness and fidgety revenge
– Gwendolyn Brooks

who am i
to judge your love
who am i
to know what your
heart swells with
what your body needs
what it feels warm against
comfortable with
to know
what eases your day
making it blithe
giving it meaning

who am i
to understand
what broken thing inside
becomes whole
when she is there

i only want your thoughts
to fit my schedule
your laughter to come into
my room
when i need it most

whatever sin
they have branded
you with
i will forgive
come home
when you want
i will not lock the door
nothing to fear
my heart is
what it has always been
a place you will find
refuge

A New Dare

i burden you with
my dreams

they weigh on you
because they are not
your dreams
but mine
always mine
even when
i envision them
for you

when you were safe
in story books and rhyme
i dreamed them for you

when all you wanted
was warmth
and cookies from a jar

now they are not
part of your plan
your agenda is full
with other cravings

i apologize
you apologize
but nothing untangles
the nature
of who we are

*

make me understand
this place you go to
that terrorizes
erases all i had designed
for us

these pitiable imaginings
i thought were
the right ones
nothing but splinters
under the skin

make me feel
what your smile
seems to know
the uncomplicated reason
for falling in love
believing it is all that matters
all that is reasonable
and real

you taunt me
with a new dare
now that the games
are done
a new defiance
too precarious to occupy

how do i master the
latest technology

seems only my pen
outlines my heart

Death on Page Three

for Nicole Ignagni

i pick up the paper
sit in the sun
a spring afternoon
makes promises

i read

a young girl
ejected
from a speeding car
an empty soda can
on the side of the road
tossed
without concern

babies on a joy ride
speed
such a young craving
to satisfy

another mother
inconsolable
tonight

It Is Murder

I have seen the future
it is murder
– Leonard Cohen

i remember the exact moment
the murder
the afternoon
an autumn day
a Sunday
in the kitchen
standing at the sink
the feeble light
through the
half raised blind
of that east facing window

delightful as always
her eyes
their Asian slant
the grace of her hands
the perfect presence of
her stance
no clue
then the smooth blade
of words
the last real kiss
the blackout

Last Stop

on a painting by Grethe Jensen

always the
saddest
that last stop
the ride
complete

the red and black
dragon
hushed
its steamy eyes
spent

Another Road

on a painting by Patsy Berton

most alluring
when it is silent

compacted and washed
by rain and time

a long continuous curve
slips through trees

infinite
unlimited

carving history without
sound or blade

The Clothesline

on a painting by Patsy Berton

Mrs. Rondinelli did laundry
every Monday and Friday
rain or shine
whatever the season

i was greeted by her
husband's socks
marching eastward
long and woolen
all in a row
pinned one by one with
wooden pegs
all facing the same direction
the blue checkered shirts followed
arms extended and free
in breezy conversation
with the early morning air
then came the pants
the polka-dotted boxers
endless procession of male apparel

the feminine under-things
reserved for a second line
girdles and sensible cottons
the flannel nightgowns
buttoned up
towels
white gleaming sheets
proudly in the middle
at the very end were the teenage panties
lace bras that belonged to her youngest

Mrs. Rondinelli would stand
for long quiet moments
arms folded under her weighty breasts
her serious eyes fixed
on the orderly clothesline
radiant in the morning light
her crisp, controlled world
clean
without intrusion

Tony's Car

on a painting by Patsy Berton

in the laneway
behind Crawford Street
between the maple and the magnolia
he'd back it up
gradually
making sure not to decapitate
the hollyhocks and geraniums
his mother had planted

stopping where the cement
bordered the grass
he'd park his new baby
turn off her lights
and lounge there a while

then he'd open the door
step out in slow motion
observe the silver shining chrome
slide his warm hand the length
of her polished cobalt blue shell
kiss his fingers
and leave her to the night

Happy Birthday

for Serena

you have survived childhood
religion
the guilt of being born
woman
the ideas of men

you are aging without consent
or rebellion

your hands never idle
with superfluous things
there is still life to live
mother's plants to tend
the watering

make the same wish
this time around
while the candles glow
the light is enticing

Hagar

on a painting by M.C. Conlon

it is always the women
angels
servants
whores
and wives

bearing sons
always sons

to inhabit the glory
the throne

occupy the sacred
passing of time

Sorella

for Antonia Pozzi (1912-1938)

"I have so much faith in you"

your first line
much to believe in
but you distrusted

what prison held you
narrowing the gaps
words
unborn
from the swell in your heart

that silence
the appetite for amity
never satisfied

odd thing you believed you were
the sadness in your mouth

a sparrow's song
enters a weightless sky

Rituzza

for Rita Atri (in dialect)

Rituzza
figlia strana
ricordati
che sei Siciliana

sempre sta' penna
in mano
st' occhi scuri
e granni
ca cercano la luce

quann a femmena
apri l'occhi
e prenne a penna
in mano
u munno piensa
che essa e'
pazza

Little Rita

(translated from the dialect)

little Rita
strange daughter
remember
you are Sicilian

always with this pen
in hand
these eyes so big
and dark
looking for the light

when a woman
opens her eyes
and takes a pen
in hand
the world thinks
she's gone
mad

Outdated

if i choose
i can pretend
not to see
turn away
cry when you're not there
accept what isn't possible
i am good at hiding things
small things
large things
but they will not stay hidden
forever

i don't know what to do with
the loss of all the
ordinary things
the babies
their birthdays

A Girl Made of Lavender

for my cousins Rose and John

i can still smell Lynne's white starched blouse
her see-through white skin glowing
as i sat in the seat next to her
at Gledhill Public School

Lynne was the first Canadian girl
i saw when i walked into Mrs. Riley's
third grade class

Lynne looked like Canada
Lynne smelled like Canada

my black uncombed curls
and homemade dress
made me feel ashamed
i was unscented
and without starch

from that first day
when i sat beside her
i wanted to be Lynne
i wanted to smell like Lynne

i learned later
her perfect starched clean blouse
was sprayed with lavender

Lynne was forever stuck
inside my nose
a girl made of lavender

Darrel and Billy were both
in love with Lynne
and she knew they were
every time she took the Jersey Milk
chocolate bars they stole for her
from Henry's five and ten cent store

it was always a contest
who could earn her love
with the sweetest candies
the best chocolate
stolen from the candy store
just for her

Billy got caught once
Henry dragged him to the principal's office
Billy's mother had to come to school
she was really mad
she screamed and yelled so loud
we could hear her down the hall

but it didn't stop Billy
he just switched stores

the next day he brought Lynne caramels
he'd picked up at Woolworth's at the corner of
Danforth and Woodbine

Darrel followed Lynne everywhere
every recess and every lunch hour
after school he'd wait by the fence
till she appeared
his eyes crammed with her white beauty
her clean ironed clothes
and her sweet smell

Sometimes Darrel brought Lynne
little glass statues of animals
wrapped in pink Kleenex
he kept them in his pocket
until Lynne appeared
then he would hand them to her
with a smile that showed all
his teeth

i wondered where he got them from
they looked expensive
but he never told anyone

every week like magic
a new animal made of glass
wrapped in pink Kleenex
came out of his pocket

Darrel loved animals
he loved horses
and drew them on big sheets
of coloured paper
they looked almost real
like pictures taken with a camera

he drew the horses for Lynne
but she preferred the little glass animals
she always threw the drawings away

Darrel and Billy lived for Lynne
other boys made fun of them
but Darrel and Billy didn't care
they guarded Lynne like a princess
protected her from anything
that didn't shine like she did
made sure she always had
plenty of sweet caramels
and glassy things to keep her company

Lynne hardly ever played with girls
she never once played with me

Lynne had tiny perfect ears
like beautiful shells from the sea
i could see them because her hair was
always in a ponytail
tied with a blue ribbon

the elastic that held my curls together
was thick and brown

Lynne's head was just the right size
i would stare at it sometimes
watch her ponytail swish back and forth
hoping that once, just once
she would turn and see me
she never did

Mrs. Riley wasn't sure
what to do with me
the day i walked into her class
she sat me next to Lynne
hoping her light would somehow
creep into me
it never did

i tried to copy everything Lynne would do
the way she sat up straight at her desk
the way she held her head up
on her skinny long neck
staring at the blackboard
even when there was nothing
on the blackboard to look at

i watched how her fingers
moved her pencil
how she printed her letters
her numbers so neatly
between the lines on the workbook page

i tried to do the same
but i never understood why
the numbers and letters
had to stay so neatly between the lines

Lynne never told me why
neither did Mrs. Riley

The day Cristina came into our room
Mrs. Riley moved me
to the back of the class
next to Brenda
who didn't have a smell at all
but was very tall

Cristina was new to Gledhill Public
she came from an island
in the middle of the ocean
a place called Greece

Mrs. Riley didn't know what to do with her
either
but she must have thought
Cristina needed Lynne more than i did
because she gave her my seat

i didn't want to move
i liked sitting next to Lynne
even if she never looked at me
or talked to me
sitting next to Lynne made me feel
that i belonged a little
sitting next to Lynne made me think
that one day
i could smell like lavender
that someday
someone would steal Jersey milk chocolate bars
just for me

i wanted to sit next to Lynne forever
but now Cristina
needed Lynne more than i did
Cristina's sad crossed eyes
told me that

i moved next to Brenda
who had no smell at all

Brenda's tall head hid Lynne's pretty ears
Brenda's hair didn't move
it just sat flat and brown
without ribbons
she chewed her fingernails
one by one
spitting the bits on the pages of
Run Spot, Run

*

It was a long walk down Danforth Avenue
to Woodbine from Gledhill Public
nobody lived as far from the school as i did
except Cristina

she lived on Aldergrove Avenue
the dead end street near the railway track
i lived on Moberly
the street that led to the railway track

Lynne lived a few houses from the school
she went home for lunch every day
her mother always waited on the veranda

Cristina and me ate our big messy sandwiches
in the school yard

Sometimes Cristina followed me home
two or three steps behind me
if i stopped she stopped
if i moved she moved
one day i just turned around
talked to her
she didn't understand me much
and i didn't understand her
but we walked together anyway

she had these funny crossed eyes
that stared at her own nose
i wanted to laugh a little
but i never did

The day Mrs. Riley left
to have her baby Lynne cried
that day Lynne looked different
when i watched tears slide down
her perfect face
leaving little wet spots
on her clean blouse
i felt really sad

i was sure that girls made of lavender
with seashell ears and ponytails
who ate Jersey Milk chocolate bars
would never have to cry

The new teacher wasn't nice like Mrs. Riley
the new teacher was full of freckles
her lips cracked at the side and
spit gathered in the tiny cracks
when she talked

the new teacher sat Cristina next to me
the last seat by the window
in the fifth row
i couldn't see Lynne anymore
from where i was sitting
i couldn't smell her
or watch her ponytail bounce
back and forth
her perfect head and sea shell ears
disappeared

Cristina's ears were big and round and
she wore a small gold loop in each one
Cristina didn't chew her fingernails
she didn't smell like lavender
she didn't look like Canada
and her hair was sort of wild

we sat together in the last two seats
of the fifth row
where nobody ever passed by
but from that day on
we walked home together
after school every day

we saved our coppers for a while
when we had saved enough
we went to Woolworth's
and bought a miniature bottle of lavender
sprayed it all over our clothes
all over our hair and skin
but we didn't smell like Lynne at all

it wasn't long before we realized
lavender
would never smell the same on
girls like us

The Fall of Rome

Risorgimento

the boys are at it again

my south
is bigger than yours!

behind the castles
or the barns
orgasms
of hand and tongue
a blade
and then
the butchery

the women wait
it will be the season of rape
soon enough

the south will rise again

*

the sadness we inherited
from ancestors
for all the reasons
that moved us around the world
the kick in the ass
the abandonment
the massacre

it should have made us
stronger
smarter
kinder

it should have brought us
closer
we should have
talked

but the bitter lingers
on self-serving lips

taste the venom
still thick
so sweet

Back in Town

I knew I was in the
wrong century
And wrongly dressed
– Ted Hughes

i am softer now
the muscles
are softer now

i have things to deal with
in another place
but i am back
one more time
giving my eyes permission
to witness the lie
indulging this half drunk
delirious heart

*

in the *piazza*
the bells of *Sant' Arduino*
are what they have always been
no interpreter needed
they keep me company
at the *caffè* table
secure in their sound
they belong here

*

the little *signora* is curious
stops at my table
without an invitation

something in her eyes
is particular to this town
the sad slant
the folded lids
the softness of brown:
my father's eyes

"why are you back
there's nothing here for you
in this miserable town
you escaped
go home where you live now
and be grateful"

i am the unexploited ear
that listens
she unloads her regrets
they fall hard
ancient as the stones
of the *vicolo*

the locals walk by
without stopping

*

every hour
the bells sound
i do not sleep
the bed
new to my curves

everywhere the smell
of musty
forgotten things
abandoned history
rotting

this town by the river
never dries
the sun in autumn
a brief fix
it cannot hide
the centuries
of decay

my Italy
each time i return
there is less of it i recognize

thank god for
the hills
not as green as i remember

the hills are still here

Bunga, Bunga

everyone speaks "Italian:"
the King's Italian
Berlusconi's Italian
slick
smooth
arrogant and banal

old words discarded
children reject the
established tunes

everything is style
outlet malls
breathing
American fiction

few real women
to court
fewer men
who can muster
the romance

a magic kiss
to wake up the heart

this is Berlusconi time
a love affair
without
love

The Fall of Rome

gluttons
ate this city
for lunch

left crumbs
for pigeons
and tourists who
gather in the *piazza*

the charm has
faded
there is greed
indifference
garbage

Fellini is dead
Pasolini is dead
so is Magnani
and the myth

there are fewer coins
in the fountain

terror wears a suit
and a tie
difficult to detect
and the child learns
the trade

art is an amulet
a counterfeit copy

the euro waits
in a long long line
into the Vatican

Heredity

the women behind the bar
have my shape
wide shoulders
on a straight trunk
thin lips
no hips
hands suited more
for turning the soil
than writing poems

they work the espresso machine
a musical instrument
their fluent fingers
pour *grappa*
without spilling a drop

Prince Edward County

for my husband

hollyhocks stand
at attention
under a mackerel sky

Wapoos Island
a giant lily pad
drifts
on Lake Ontario

Bruce Cockburn
hitches a ride
along interstate 81
while we head east
to visit the loyalists

we'll pour the new
county wines
toast another summer
another moon
another flight
maybe get a little drunk

Pier 21/Halifax, Nova Scotia

it is my anniversary

after fifty years
i visit a port
where a ship once docked

a cemetery
of names on bricks

photographs of faces
in distress
toy ships with detail
cardboard suitcases
hold nothing
frayed wool caps
positioned on hooks

some of us have come
to walk to the gravesite
read ourselves
into the past
hoping to understand
something profound
recognize something
special

all i can recall is water
and a belly upside down

here is where i landed
fifty summers ago
but this is another place
now

When You're 64

for Philip Conlon

Philip our first home
has forgotten us

we raced out the back door
with all those ideals
inside our pockets
the little red book
of hope
Dylan on the radio
revolution

was it the seventies
or earlier than that
it's all a little blurry now

your American accent
Brooklyn or the Bronx
that giant poster of Verdi
on your kitchen wall
Gramsci and Marx
on the table

did we really want
to change the world
from Dufferin and St. Clair

we ate *gelato*
while Bobby Sands starved

remember Nicaragua
Victor Jara
Violeta's ode to life

and Viet Nam
remember Viet Nam

was it all so long ago
when
change was promising

from the Empire State
now
Manhattan
has a sad new skyline

Remembering Swans

for Bub Bridger

"remember?
Their wild cries
and those white white
wingtips flashing"

living up there
at the very top
overlooking the airport
among the hydrangea
and roses
eyes crammed
with sky and sea
hair careless
in that Wellington wind
those green waves
undulating
watching swans
their perfection

on a bench
at Oriental Parade
hills in my eyes
gulls in my ears
i remember you
remembering

The Garden on Kaka Street

for Ena and Gia

there's a photo of nana
and you
under the pear tree
in the Kaka Street garden
you are three
nana is old

you climb the low branches
determined
she holds her arm out
to protect you

the pears you pull
will be sliced
eaten with cheese
at suppertime
after the ham and the
kumara

you will want them with
ice cream
vanilla

you don't climb trees
anymore
you haven't climbed them
in years

you don't eat fruit much
either
especially not pears
but i slice them still
hide them in ice cream

while some other child
learns to climb
fruit trees

Otaki Hills

for Robin and Stuart

so much of who i am
is made up of hills

their morning whisper
their midday sleep

their blue lullaby
under that long white cloud

Rainy Day/notes with wine

1.
when you are feeling ugly
and fat
and foolish
and unnecessary
it always seems to be
raining

2.
my heart is bigger than
my head
i wish it was the other way
around

3.
my friends who are writers
are all men
deep thinkers
i don't know where the women are
perhaps they're reading
some are ironing

4.
it is the nature of the duality
light-darkness
good-evil
senseless to seek
redemption
or even understanding
we are doomed to the
duel

A Found Poem in the Globe and Mail

"I am driven by three things:
I know who I am; I know what
I'm here to do and I know who

I'm here to serve."
– Julian Fantino, *Globe and Mail*, Dec. 4, 2010

Lucky Julian!

The Boys Are Beautiful

for Christian and the men at Caritas

wounded as they are
outside
the stitches are internal

i bring them my
small scratches
on occasion
in a neat package
of white paper
printed and bound

i read them my life
among the metaphors

as young as they are
they find their link

Christian might have been
my son
if i had had a son

gathered beneath the maple
of an Ontario countryside
so many lives suspended
by what should have been
the grace of youth

it's a long way back
from the joy ride
to mamma's arms

we are here
to learn to
love ourselves again
or maybe for
the first time

The Old Man Next Door

it isn't pretty
what passing time
sculpts

the old man next door
stooped
mumbling to himself
unshaved
unwashed
tearing at my flowers
snipping the branches
of my tree that dared
cross his line
cursing the green
the cherries
and me
as he waters the cement
he has poured and smoothed
with confidence

the water becomes a river
over his grey
unyielding masterpiece
that will last forever

spiteful old man
next door
wrestles with time
pruning his fear
and my innocuous
hushed
little city garden

A Fool in a Straw Hat

each time i come back
they rob me again
as if the first theft
was not enough

they see the fool
in the straw hat
returning
too many suitcases
and unstable knees
a purse full of memory
ready for emptying

the wallet goes easily
the money, the cards
only paper

in the indifferent
hands of thieves
i have no history
here

Saints and Beads

they hang around my neck
my wrists
hide in my pockets
between my breasts
amulets
for protection
powerless
against the skill
of Neapolitan *zingari*
whose ingenious fingers
rival the masters
the sculptors
the painters
who once honoured
this land

Poets of Water and Wilderness

for Atwood and Musgrave

Margaret and Susan have come
to *Procida* on paper

Canadian mermaids
ocean goddesses
rising from the seas
and dark lakes

enchanting creatures
who mesmerize
take the reader to a land
of mystery and space

they distract *paesani*
from their own sea fish gods
who have been caught
for centuries
in the seaweed of indifference
left quietly to drown
in unfamiliar waters

Procida, the Island

for Oriana

we are sleeping in Sofia's bed
the young concierge tells us
it is the room she requests
each time she comes to the island
just a short boat ride from *Pozzuoli*
where she was born

the balcony looks down on the marina
where Troisi met Neruda
and traded metaphors
for his final performance

men were exiled here
walls too tall to escape from
sea everywhere
lemons large as suns

something in this beauty
the calm
blue mystery
and passing time
makes you hopeful

The Turnabout

the landscape i used to dream about
does not hug me anymore
like my grown daughter
it does not feel the need

i resist falling into sentiment
cannot stay long anyway
always less than the time before

this place is almost done
the rhythm here is bad
for my heart

Addò Stà La Chiau

(Cepranese dialect)
for Peppe Nalli

sò remenuta
alla casa de 'ste paese
ma la porta de legne e ferre
la sò truata chiusa

pe' raprirla
ce uleua chella chiau
longa e nera
che pesaua miese chile

chissà addò a ita a feni?
starà attaccata a ca chiode
'nfaccia a ca mure
pe'ricordo o fantasia,
attaccata come a chella
fotografia bianca e nera
che mamma tè
dentre alla cucina:
le cantamesse n'ciocca
a 'na pupetta
ustuta de bianche
chi petaline tutte de merlette

Where Is the Key

(translated from Cepranese dialect)

i came home
to the house in this town
but the door of wood and steel
was locked

i needed the key
the long black one
that weighed half a kilo
to open that door

who knows where it ended up
maybe it's hanging on a nail
on some wall
a memory or a fantasy
pinned
like that black and white photograph
mamma has in the kitchen

the *cantamesse* on the heads
of the little girls
in white dresses
and lace socks

Terra Murata

i pretend to be comfortable
in my company
alone on this island
where i have come
to share my life
my poems
in an abandoned church
that has changed objective
a hall of study
where our journeys meet

waiting for the doors to open
i am early
something i attribute to the
Canadian in me
everyone is still lunching
long, long lunches here

i am parked on a stoop
next to a colossal wall
no one has ever climbed

between the sun
and cool dampness
that lives in stone
homeless cats lie careless
and quiet around me
i would tell them of my
abandonment
but they aren't interested

the only other sound
is the incessant cooing
of pigeons and doves
an irritation
with time

L'Altra Italia Lives Here

dropped in
by invitation only

another Villa in Woodbridge
marble pillars
at the gate
vespas
on the cobbled drive
fountains without coins

Michelangelo's David
lies glittering
in mosaic
at the bottom of the pool
twelve feet long

chefs catering
prosecco bubbling
and wine, wine,
                    wine

beautiful wives
strewn about
Brazilian waxed
and bronzed

the men light the cigars

Ah life in Canada!
dolce

the other *Italia*
lives here
and doing just fine

cin cin!

The Gambler's Daughter

for Father Gianni

the gambler You are
reminds me of my father
he never had much luck
had no time for You at all
left the prayers to mamma
and me

i have learned them all
backwards and forwards
mamma can even sing them
in Latin
and she does
incessantly

her beads have changed more
than colour in a lifetime
she believes in You still
without argument
something about love
and family
keep her strong

i am the one You torment
keep testing

which card to play this time around
love, death, pain
the big "C"
here comes another loss
there goes another flower
appropriated
for Your estate
i am left to re-pot the space
reorganize

i never liked to gamble
found it sad
desperate
like papa's eyes when he lost

but You dwell in it
defeat makes you stronger
how is that?

i'm picking up the beads tonight
the red crystal ones
join mamma on the couch
hoping i'll get lucky
stay tough

ACKNOWLEDGEMENTS

As always, my gratitude to my amazing family who won't give up on me.

Thank-you to Beatriz Hausner for your insights and to the Quattro Books team (Allan, John, Luciano) for your continuing support.

To Rob Marra for his gift of painting.

To my friends without whom the laughter would be limited and the wine less intoxicating.

To all who have come in and out of my life giving the words their meaning.

To Italy, Canada, and New Zealand, my trinity.

Grazie a Giuseppe Nalli che mi aiuta a ritrovare la lingua.

To Andrew for his love and award-winning patience.

Much love,

Gianna Patriarca